HARBHAJAN SINGH COLOUR

MR VIVEK KUMAR PANDEY
SHAMBHUNATH

ISBN 979-888530689-8

Short biography of Harbhajan Singh and about life .During writing this book no character & no religious are harmed written by Mr Vivek Kumar Pandey. winner youngest writer award 1st rank in india 2020.He is only one writer can publish 700+ own book that was greatest successfull in his life.This book fully colour edition books.

Contents

Foreword

Author biography in English :MY NAME IS VIVEK KUMAR PANDEY . I WAS BORN IN 30 SEP 2002,I AM FROM SURAT GUJARAT INDIA.MY DREAM WAS TO BE GOOD WRITERS ,MY FAMILY SUPPORTED ME TO SUCCESSFUL AND I CAN DO IT MY SELF.How do I write? That is a question, I believe, that cannot be honestly answered by me."CELEBRATING YOUNGEST WRITER AWARD WINNER IN GUJARAT 1ST RANK" MR PANDEY JI . I may think I did a good job writing something when in reality it could be horrible. The reader is the one who decides the quality of my writing. I do not find writing to be natural to me and therefore find it to be a real challenge. My trick as a challenged writer is to do the best I can and know that I am happy with the final outcome. It may take a while to do my best and there may be quite a few problems I run into along the way.

I am not a greedy person those who are thinking about me and my self I never tried it anyone people suffering from sadness ,I trying to get promoted people suffering from happiness and joy in your Life Time. Now in current situation in India and also world people are unemployed and have no many but our indian governor help to people to get free food from ration card , i also take part in leadership team ,i am Motivational speaker , Film script writer. There was my two dream firstly writer and secondly actor & also my own film is upcoming soon i done almost completely completed script for my film .I AM GOING TO SAY WORD OF HEART TOUCH OUT PLEASE READ IT" , firstly i thanks my father he supports me in this field they always getting inspired me by own his words and behavior ,they always said that he was a biggest person in the world in future and also they purchase fruit and chocolate for me in anytime & anyway , firstly my father buy him then call me Vivek you want a chocolate i will say yes papa but how many tell me ,papa: you tell me how much i buy him i told 1 or 2 chocolate but my father purchase whole the boxes of chocolate and they get suprised me. MY FATHER WAS BORN IN " 20 SEPTEMBER" 1971 IN INDIA.

1) MY FATHER FAVORITE CLOTHES IS KURTA PAIJMA AND ALSO STYLES SHOE

2) FAVORITE SINGER IS KISHORE DA

3) FAVORITE STATE GUJARAT AND KOLKATA , HIS VILLAGE IN BIHAR

4) FAVORITE COLOR BLACK AND WHITE

THEY ALSO LOVE cricket like IPL and one day t-20 .they also like watching a News daily and heard the song daily ,they also interested in tik tok video but in current time tik tok is banned in india but also few videos are in you tube. In lockdown time my family and me very enjoy day daily. my father play daily ludo with his sister and son, daughter.they always loved tea and coffee anytime call me "। विविके थोड़ा चाय बनाओना विविके तुम्हारे हाथ का चाय अच्छा लगता है". I make it tea for my father but some reason after the April to june they are suffering from fever and cough , weakness on 6 June 2020 my father death. they not told me say bye bye his life. After death of 6 June on 10 june my mom and dad anniversary.but my father is Best in the world they can do anything for me please take care of father and respect it of your parents.

CHAPTER ONE

Harbhajan Singh Colour

- Harbhajan Singh

> *"During writing this book no character & no religious are harmed written by Mr Vivek Kumar Pandey.Short Bio Of Indian Cricketer."*

Harbhajan Singh (born 3 July 1980) is an Indian cricketer and cricket commentator who has played all formats of cricket for India. A specialist spinner, he has the Fourth-highest number of Test wickets by an off-spinner behind India's Ravichandran Ashwin and Sri Lanka's Muttiah Muralitharan and Rangana Herath.

Singh was captain of IPL team Mumbai Indians and Punjab for the 2012–13 Ranji Trophy season. Under his captaincy, Mumbai Indians won the 2011 Champions League Twenty20.

Singh made his Test and One Day International (ODI) debuts in early 1998. His career was initially affected by investigations into the legality of his bowling action, as well as several disciplinary incidents. However, in 2001, with leading leg spinner Anil Kumble injured, Harbhajan's career was resuscitated after Indian captain Sourav Ganguly called for his inclusion in the Border-Gavaskar Trophy team. In that series victory over Australia, Harbhajan established himself as the team's leading spinner by taking 32 wickets, becoming the first Indian bowler to take a hat-trick in Test cricket.Post his 2001 cricket performance, he was offered, by

Government of Punjab, a role of a Deputy Superintendent of Police, in Punjab Police, but due to its non-compliance by Harbhajan Singh, same was later withdrawn.

A finger injury in mid-2003 sidelined Singh for much of the following year, allowing Kumble to regain his position as the first choice spinner in Tests and ODIs. Harbhajan reclaimed a regular position in the team upon his return in late 2004, but often found himself watching from the sidelines in Test matches outside the Indian subcontinent with typically only one spinner, Kumble, being used. Throughout 2006 and into early 2007, his accumulation of wickets fell and his bowling average increased, and he was increasingly criticised for bowling defensively with less loop.

Following India's first-round elimination from the 2007 Cricket World Cup, his was replaced by other spinners in the national squad for both formats. He regained a regular position in the team in late 2007, but became the subject of more controversy. In early 2008, he was given a ban by the International Cricket Council (ICC) for racially vilifying Andrew Symonds. The ban was revoked upon appeal, but in April, he was banned from the 2008 Indian Premier League and suspended from the ODI team by the Board of Control for Cricket in India (BCCI) for slapping Sreesanth after a match. He appeared in Total Nonstop Action Wrestling's Indian promotion, Ring Ka King. He was in the World Cup-winning team of 2011 Cricket World Cup.Singh was conferred the Padma Shri, India's fourth highest civilian honour, in 2009.

- Early years and personal life

Harbhajan Singh was born into a Sikh family. He is the only son of Sardar Sardev Singh Plaha, a businessman who owned a ball bearing and valve factory. Growing up with five sisters, Harbhajan was in line to inherit the family business, but his father insisted that he concentrate on his cricket career and represent India.

Harbhajan was trained as a batsman by his first coach Charanjit Singh Bhullar, but converted to spin bowling after his coach's untimely death saw him turn to the tutelage of Davinder Arora. Arora credits Harbhajan's success to a work ethic that included a three-hour training session in the morning, followed by an afternoon session lasting from 3 PM until after sunset.

Following the death of his father in 2000, Harbhajan became the family head, and by 2001 had organised marriages for three of his sisters. In 2002 he ruled out his own marriage until at least 2008. In 2005 he again fended off marriage rumours linking him to a Bangalore-based bride, stating that he would only make a decision "after a couple of years", and that he would be seeking a Punjabi bride selected by his family. In a country where cricketers are idolised, Harbhajan's performances have brought him government accolades and lucrative sponsorships. Following his performance against Australia in 2001, the Government of Punjab awarded him 5 lakhs, a plot of land, and an offer to become a Deputy Superintendent of Police in Punjab Police, which he did not comply (accept) later.

Despite having a job offer with the constabulary, Harbhajan sustained minor injuries in March 2002 in an altercation with police outside the team hotel in Guwahati. The scuffle broke out when Harbhajan remonstrated with officers after they refused to allow a photographer into the hotel. Harbhajan cut his bowling arm and injured his elbow when he was struck by the police. Extensive negotiations from local officials and organisers were required to dissuade Harbhajan and captain Sourav Ganguly from leaving the area after Ganguly said that the Indian team would abandon the scheduled match against Zimbabwe.

Singh was caught at Auckland airport for failing to declare that he had filthy boots in his luggage. His only excuse was that he "couldn't be bothered" complying with New Zealand quarantine laws. He was fined $200 on the spot.

One of his common nicknames, outside India, is The Turbanator, deriving from his skill as a bowler in terminating the innings of the opposing team, and the fact that, as a Sikh, he wears a turban whenever he plays. Among Indians, Harbhajan is more commonly known as bhajji.[8] It was estimated in 2005 that Harbhajan was the most recognised and commercially viable Indian cricketer after Sachin Tendulkar, in part due to his colourful personality and iconic turban, as well as his reputation for enjoying the celebrity social scene. His signing for English county team Surrey in 2005, based at The Oval in London, was partly attributed to his marketability. Harbhajan had generated a large personal following in the western London suburb of Southall, which boasts a majority Punjabi Sikh population, when he lived there in 1998 while training under Fred Titmus.

- Singh with wife Geeta Basra at Rakesh Roshan's birthday bash in 2017

In 2006 Harbhajan's endorsements generated controversy when he appeared without his turban in an advertisement for Royal Stag whisky. This angered many orthodox Sikhs, leading to anti-Harbhajan protests in the Sikh holy city of Amritsar, with effigies of Harbhajan being burnt. The Sikh clergy and Shiromani Gurdwara Prabandhak Committee demanded an apology from him and asked Seagram's to withdraw the advert, on the basis that it had "hurt the feelings of Sikhs". Harbhajan quickly issued an apology, but he was also unhappy at the clergy's interference, stating "If they were unhappy, they should have called me and talked to me like a son".

Harbhajan Singh married his longtime girlfriend, actress Geeta Basra, on 29 October 2015 in Jalandhar. They have a daughter, born on 27 July 2016, and a son, born on 10 July 2021.

- Domestic career

Harbhajan broke into the Punjab Under-16s at the age of 15 years and 4 months in November of the 1995–96 season, and took 7/46 and 5/138 on debut against Haryana, setting up a nine-wicket win. He scored 56 in his next match against Delhi and then took 11/79 in his third match against Himachal Pradesh, orchestrating an innings win. He ended with 32 wickets at 15.15 and 96 runs at 48.00 in four matches. He was rewarded with selection for North Zone Under-16s, a team that represents all of northern India for a one-day series, in which he took two wickets at 43.50 in four matches and scored 18 runs. At the end of the season, he was called into the national Under-19 team at the age of 15 years and 9 months for a youth One Day International against South Africa. He took 1/19 from seven overs in an Indian win.

In 1996–97, Harbhajan was promoted to the Punjab Under-19s and he took 15 wickets at 20.20 in three matches, although he managed only two runs with the bat. This included match figures of 8/54 in an innings win over Jammu and Kashmir.

Harbhajan made his first-class cricket debut in late 1997 against Services, during the 1997–98 Ranji Trophy season. He took a total of 3/35 in an innings win but was dropped back to the Under-19s the following week. He then took 5/75 and 7/44 in two matches to earn a recall to the senior team. He then took a total of 7/123 in the next two matches for Punjab to earn selection for North Zone in the Duleep Trophy.

Harbhajan's season was interrupted when he represented India at the Under-19 World Cup in January 1998. He played in six matches, taking eight wickets at 24.75 with a best of 3/5 against Kenya.

Returning to India he played in three more Ranji Trophy matches, and from a total of six matches, he took 18 wickets at an average of 22.50, ranking outside the top 20 in wicket taking. He took a total of 5/131 as North lost to East Zone by five wickets.

Harbhajan played the full 2009 Indian Premier League season in South Africa, taking 12 wickets at 21.33 and an economy rate of 5.81 in 13 matches. He was one of the most economical bowlers in the competition, and took 1/9 in four overs against Punjab to win the man of the match award. He ended the season with 4/17 against Delhi, but it was not enough to prevent a four-wicket defeat.

During the 2010 IPL season, he finished as the Mumbai Indian's leading wicket taker with 17 victims at an average of 22.17 helping his team to reach the final. Harbhajan opened the bowling during the final vs Chennai Super Kings but went wicketless and was promoted as a pinch hitter to number 4 in the batting order but could only contribute 1 run in the defeat.

Harbhajan had a largely successful 2011 IPL as part of an effective Mumbai Indians bowling attack. He took 5 for 18 against Chennai Super Kings during the round robin part of the tournament which are the best bowling figures of any player at the Wankhede Stadium in the IPL However, the team's form faltered during the playoffs as they lost back to back matches to Kolkata Knight Riders and Chennai Super Kings to miss out on the final.

After injuries, he returned to competitive cricket to lead the Mumbai Indians to 2011 Champions League Twenty20 title, but fell out of favor with the national selectors. He was not chosen in the home series squad against England in October and West Indies in November and December. Mumbai Indians won their first ever championship under his captaincy, winning the Champions League by 31 runs. Harbhajan was man of the match for his contribution.

He went to play the IPL 2012 which was not that successful for him, but took his team to semi final while being captain. Harbhajan went to play for Essex in England but is not selected for the Sri Lankan tour before the 2012 ICC World Twenty20. In his debut match for Essex against Gloucestershire, Harbhajan did not take any wicket on 12 July 2012, conceding 33 runs in his 12 overs. He was bought by Chennai Super Kings in 2018 after 10 years with Mumbai Indians.On 20 January 2021 Harbajan announced his contract ended with Chennai Super Kings. He was signed by Kolkata Knight Riders during the 2021 IPL auction for a sum of 2 crore.

- Doorstep to international arena

After taking eight wickets in his next two Ranji matches, Harbhajan was selected to tour Australia in 1999–2000, as the second spinner. He did not play in the Tests, with India opting to field only Anil Kumble in the team. Australia whitewashed India 3–0, and Harbhajan struggled in his only first-class outing against Tasmania, taking 0/141, a portent of future unsuccessful tours to Australia.

Harbhajan was not part of the ODI squad for the Australian tour and upon returning to India in early 2000 needed strong first-class results to maintain his Test position. He went wicketless against Hyderabad, and was selected for the Board President's XI match against the touring South Africans. He took 2/88 and 2/59 and scored 38 and 39 to prevent the hosts being bowled out and defeated, but was dropped as the second slow bowler, as Murali Kartik became Kumble's spinning partner. Harbhajan returned to domestic action, taking 24 wickets in Punjab's remaining four first-class matches. He ended the Indian season with 46 first-class wickets at 26.23.

In mid-2000 an opportunity arose when Harbhajan was selected in the first group of trainees sent to the National Cricket Academy to study under Erapalli Prasanna and Srinivas Venkataraghavan, two off spin bowlers from the Indian spin quartet of the 1970s. However, his behaviour did not conform to requirements, and he was expelled on disciplinary grounds. His sponsorship job with Indian Airlines was also reviewed as a result of his indiscipline.Harbhajan later admitted that he had been at fault earlier in his career.

Following his run-ins with Indian cricket administrators, there was nothing to indicate that Harbhajan's chances of national selection had improved at the start of 2000–01. Despite Kumble being injured, Harbhajan was again overlooked as Kartik, Sunil Joshi, and debutant Sarandeep Singh were entrusted with the spin bowling duties in Test matches against Bangladesh and Zimbabwe on the subcontinent.

During the first half of the season, still in international exile, Harbhajan continued to pick up wickets on the domestic circuit. In five Ranji Trophy matches, he claimed 28 wickets at 13.96. He claimed 3/29 and 3/39 against Himachal Pradesh, 2/53 and 5/

88 against Jammu and Kashmir, 4/77 and 2/33 against Haryana and 5/40 against Services in the first four matches, all of which ended in innings wins for Punjab. He then took a total of 4/32 in a 199-run win over Delhi. Harbhajan's batting, which had rarely been productive up to this point in his career, also improved. He scored a career-best 84 against Haryana and added 52 against Services, aggregating 207 runs at 51.75. After taking eight wickets at 21.12 in six one-dayers, Harbhajan was selected for North in the Duleep Trophy, but his early-season form deserted him. He took five wickets at 39.00 in two matches, although he did continue his productive run with the bat, scoring 130 runs at 32.50 with three scores above 35. In October 2019, Harbhajan drafted his name into the Hundred at a base price of $100,000, risking his international retirement.

- International career
- Debut days

Despite the superior statistics of other bowlers in domestic cricket, Harbhajan was the selected for the Indian Board President's XI to play the touring Australian cricket team ahead of the Tests. He managed only 1/127, and was ignored for the first two Tests before being selected to make his Test debut in the Third Test against Australia in Bangalore, where he scored 4 not out and a duck, and recorded the modest match figures of 2/136 as Australia won the match by eight wickets. He was subsequently overlooked for the triangular ODI tournament in India that followed the Tests, involving Zimbabwe in addition to Australia, but was selected for all group matches in the triangular tournament that followed soon after in Sharjah, where he made his ODI debut against New Zealand. He took 1/32 from ten overs on debut as India narrowly won by 15 runs. He then took 3/41 in the next match, a defeat against Australia, but then struggled in the second qualifying match against the same team, taking 1/63 in eight overs. He was subsequently dropped for the final against Australia, which India won, and ended the series with five wickets at 33.20 at an economy rate of 4.36.

- 1997- Struggling form

Having made little success in this phase of his international career, averaging 37.75 per Test wicket to date, and overlooked by selectors, Harbhajan faced a difficult decision. His father had recently died; as the family's only son, Harbhajan was now obliged to support his mother and unmarried sisters. He contemplated quitting cricket and moving to the United States to drive trucks for a living. After being out of the team for more than 12 months, there was little overt indication of the sudden rise that would occur in his cricketing career only a few months later.

Harbhajan was then omitted from the team during a home triangular ODI tournament against Bangladesh and Kenya, after taking 0/18 from four overs in his only match of the tournament against the former opponent, but was recalled for the Singer Trophy in Sri Lanka and also involving New Zealand. Playing in all five matches, Harbhajan claimed eight wickets at an average of 24.12 and economy of 4.38 in this tournament, taking at least one scalp in each match. Harbhajan was retained for the final and took 1/57, his worst return for the series, in an Indian win. After being omitted for the Sahara Cup series against Pakistan in Toronto, Harbhajan played in a weakened Indian team at the 1998 Commonwealth Games in Kuala Lumpur, Malaysia. The matches were not given ODI status by the ICC, and India chose to send their better players to the Sahara Cup instead. India won their first two matches against Antigua and Canada, but Harbhajan managed only a total of 1/48 from 11 overs. The Indians then needed to beat a full-strength Australian outfit to win their group and progress to the semi-finals. Harbhajan was punished and went wicketless, conceding 50 runs in eight overs as Australia won by 146 runs, knocking India out of contention.

- *Recall to the team*

Harbhajan was then recalled to the first-choice team and took five wickets at an average of 22.60 at 3.89 runs an over from three matches on a tour to Zimbabwe, in what would prove to be his last ODI appearances for India for more than two years. In all, he took 18 ODI wickets at an average of 27.2 during the 1998.

After taking 2/38 and 3/60 in an innings win in a tour match, Harbhajan was retained in the Test team, taking 2/42 and 3/63 in the only Test on the Zimbabwe tour. He was unbeaten on 15 in the second innings as the final wicket fell and India succumbed to a 51-run defeat.

Returning to India, Harbhajan started the 1998–99 domestic season well, taking 3/54 and 5/39 in an innings win over Services, before following up with 6/69 and 1/93 in the next match against Delhi, claiming his first five-wicket innings haul. He then took 6/63 and scored 31 in the first innings of a match for the Board PResident's XI against a touring West Indies A, and was taken on the tour of New Zealand in December. In a tour match against Central Districts, Harbhajan struggled, aggregating 2/112. He only played in one Test during the tour, and went wicketless, conceding 72 runs.Upon returning to India, he took a total of 3/158 for India A in a match against the touring Pakistanis ahead of the Tests. After being omitted for the First Test lost in Chennai, he was recalled for the latter two matches against Pakistan, and took five wickets at 34.60 as the matches were split.He then took 3/127 in a high-scoring draw against Sri Lanka. In all, he claimed 13 wickets at an average of 36.8 in five Tests for the season. When he was free of international fixtures for the season, he played in the Ranji Trophy matches, claiming 27 wickets at an average of 24.59 in five matches, including his first five-wicket haul at first-class level. He also registered his maiden first-class fifty, scoring an unbeaten 67 against Tamil Nadu cricket team.

Harbhajan took four wickets at 33.00 during the one-dayers during the season and was overlooked for the ODI team for the whole season and missed selection for the 1999 Cricket World Cup.In September 2003, he played for India A in a one-day series against their Australian counterparts in Los Angeles. Harbhajan took eight wickets at 17.00 at 3.77 runs an over in the five matches, with a best of 3/38.

After taking 4/91 against the touring team for the Board President's XI at the start of the season, Harbhajan managed to retain his Test position for the late 1999 home series against New Zealand, as India fielded a three-pronged spin attack on dusty tracks, taking six wickets at an average of 32.66 as the hosts prevailed 1–0 in the two Tests.

- *2001 Border-Gavaskar Trophy*
- *Harbhajan bowling in the nets*

With Kumble injured before the home series in March 2001 against the visiting Australians, Harbhajan, whose previous best Test figures were only 3/30, was the only capped spinner in the Indian team for the First Test.He had been recalled after captain Sourav Ganguly publicly called for his inclusion in the team. He was to lead the spin attack against an Australian team which had set a world record with 16 consecutive Test victories, and was searching for its first series victory on Indian soil since 1969. In a warm-up match for India A, Harbhajan had taken 2/63 and 3/81 against the tourists.

Harbhajan started well in the First Test in Mumbai, taking three quick wickets in a spell of 3/8, to reduce Australia to 99/5 in response to India's first innings of 176. However, a counter-attacking 197-run partnership between Matthew Hayden and Adam Gilchrist in just 32 overs, saw Harbhajan concede 103 runs from his last 17 overs, to end with 4/121. Despite being struck for many sixes into the crowd, it was still Harbhajan's best statistical analysis at Test level. Australia eventually proceeded to a crushing 10-wicket victory, their sixteenth consecutive Test victory in succession. This test match has been called by many the greatest that has ever been played, in light of the nature of India's win under difficult circumstances.

With leading paceman Javagal Srinath ruled out of the series with a finger injury during the First Test, the teams met for the Second Test in Kolkata, with an even bigger burden on Harbhajan. Public opinion was skeptical about India's chances of stopping Australia's winning streak, with former captain Bishan Bedi lamenting the demise of Indian cricket. Australia were again in control on the first day, having scored 193/1, with Hayden having struck Harbhajan out of the attack. Harbhajan fought back to reduce Australia to 252/7, taking five wickets in the final session, including Ricky Ponting, Gilchrist and Shane Warne in successive balls to become the first Indian to claim a Test hat-trick. After a prolonged wait for the third umpire to adjudicate whether Sadagoppan Ramesh had managed to catch Warne before the ball hit the ground, the near-capacity crowd at Eden Gardens erupted when he was given out. Harbhajan eventually finished with 7/123 as Australia were bowled out for 445.

India batted poorly and were forced to follow-on, but a 376-run partnership between V. V. S. Laxman and Rahul Dravid, who batted together for an entire day, allowed India to set Australia an imposing target of 384 to win on the final day. Australia appeared to be safely batting out the match for a draw, until losing 7/56 in the final session, collapsing from 166/3 to be bowled out for 212. Harbhajan claimed four of the wickets, to finish with 6/73 for the innings and a match tally of 13/196. India ended Australia's 16-match world record winning streak, and became only the third team to win a Test after being forced to follow on (Australia having lost all three of those matches).

The teams arrived in Chennai for the deciding Third Test, and Australia's batsmen again seized control after winning the toss, reaching 340/3 on the second morning. Then, Australian captain Steve Waugh padded away a delivery from Harbhajan. The ball spun back into Waugh's stumps, who pushed the ball away with his glove, becoming only the sixth batsman in Tests to be given out "handled the ball". Waugh's dismissal instigated another Australian batting collapse, losing 6 wickets for 51 runs to be bowled out for 391, with Harbhajan taking all six in a spell of 6/26, to finish with 7/133. After India's batsmen gained a first-innings lead of 110, the Australian batsmen were again unable to cope with Harbhajan in the second innings, who took 8/84 to end with match figures of 15/217. India appeared to be heading for an easy victory at 101/2 chasing 155, before losing 6/50 to be 151/8. Harbhajan walked to the crease, and struck the winning runs.

He was named man of the match and man of the series, having taken 32 wickets at 17.03 for the series, when none of his teammates managed more than three. The Wisden 100 study conducted by Wisden in 2002 rated all four of Harbhajan's efforts in the Second and Third Tests in the top 100 bowling performances of all time, the most for any bowler. He paid tribute to his father, who had died just six months earlier. His performance led to him usurping Anil Kumble's position as India's first-choice spinner.

- *Poor form and returning*

Harbhajan's Test success saw him recalled to the ODI team after more than two years. He was unable to reproduce his Test form against Australia, managing only four wickets at an average of 59.25 and economy rate of 5.04. His best performance was a 3/37 in a 118-run win in the third match, and a cameo batting performance of 46 runs from 34 balls, including three sixes, in a losing run chase in the fourth fixture. He was dropped from the ODI team during a subsequent triangular tournament in Zimbabwe in 2001 after only managing two wickets at 69.00 in four matches although he had been economical at 3.63 runs an over.Harbhajan was also unable to maintain his form in the Test series against Zimbabwe. Harbhajan began the tour well with 13 wickets in two warm-up matches, including a match haul of 10/80 against the CFX Academy, but could not repeat such performances in the Tests. He took eight wickets at 29.12 in the two-Test series, which was drawn 1–1, but did manage to post his first Test half-century, reaching 66 in the First Test in Bulawayo, before scoring 31 in the first innings of the Second Test as the Indian batsmen struggled and ceded their series lead. The Indians subsequently toured Sri Lanka in mid-2001, enjoying spinning wickets similar to those in India.

Harbhajan managed to establish himself in the ODI team with eleven wickets at 21.18 at the low economy rate of 3.42 in seven matches in the ODI tournament with the hosts and New Zealand. Ironically however, his best performances, in which he conceded less than 30 runs in his ten overs three times, all ended in Indian defeats. In contrast to his ODI improvement, Harbhajan's Test form deteriorated further, yielding only four wickets at 73.00 in three Tests, while Sri Lankan spinner Muttiah Muralitharan was named man of the series with 23 wickets, in what was billed as a contest between the world's two leading off-spinners. With the Tests locked at 1–1 Harbhajan managed only 2/185 in the Third Test as the hosts accumulated 6/610 declared and won by an innings. He scored 79 runs at 15.80 for the series.

Harbhajan was omitted from the Indian team in favour of Kumble as the first-choice spinner on the following tour of South Africa, only playing in the later matches when India fielded two spinners. Nevertheless, Harbhajan continued to do well in the ODIs, taking nine wickets at 20.44 in six matches at an economy rate of 3.53, winning his first man of the match award in the ODI form in an ODI against South Africa in Bloemfontein after taking 3/27 from his ten overs.He scored 62 runs at 15.50, including a rearguard 37 that was not enough to prevent an embarrassing 70-run loss to Kenya.

After being omitted for the First Test, which India lost, his disciplinary problems continued when he was one of four Indian players fined and given a suspended one match suspension for dissent and attempting to intimidate the umpire by over-appealing in the Second Test.India managed to draw the match, but Harbhajan struggled and took 1/89 and 2/79. The off spinner continued his poor overseas Test form in what would have been the Third Test. However, India defied the ICC by playing banned batsman Virender Sehwag, while Mike Denness, the match referee who handed down the penalties, was locked out of the stadium, so the match was stripped of Test status. Harbhajan continued to be ineffective, taking only 1/104, although he showed resistance with the bat, scoring 29 and 30 when many specialist batsmen failed, as India slumped to an innings defeat.

Harbhajan's Test fortunes improved immediately upon the start of the 2001–02 international season in India. Playing in his first international match at his home ground in Mohali, Punjab, Harbhajan took match figures of 7/110, including 5/51 in the first innings, to help India win the First Test by ten wickets against the touring English team. He continued his steady form throughout the series with another five wicket haul in the Second Test in Ahmedabad, to end with thirteen wickets at 24.53 for the series, although he went wicketless in 27.1 overs in the Third and final Test. Harbhajan's good home form persisted in the Test matches against Zimbabwe, taking twelve wickets at 19.66 in two games. In the First Test, he took 4/46 in the second innings to seal an innings victory after going wicketless in the second innings. His 2/70 and 6/62 in the Second Test in Delhi saw him named man of the match in a Test for the second time in his career. As in the first instance, he hit the winning runs, a straight-driven six, after India had lost six wickets and threatened to collapse in pursuit of a modest 122 for victory.He also performed strongly in the ODIs during the Indian season, taking twenty wickets at 19.75 in ten matches and taking his first five wicket haul in ODIs.In the five matches against England, he took ten wickets at 20.10 at an economy rate of 4.27. His best result was a 5/43 in the last of these matches, but a late collapse handed the tourists a five-run win. He did better against the Zimbabweans, taking 10 wickets in five matches at an average of 19.40 and an economy rate of 4.06. This included a 4/33 in the final match. He also scored 39 runs without defeat for the series, including a 24 not out as India were skittled for 191 in one match. As Harbhajan was ensconced in the Indian team for the first team, he only played in two RAnji Trophy matches for Punjab, taking 13 wickets at 20.01 and scoring 71 runs at 17.75.

Harbhajan's overseas difficulties returned during the tour of the West Indies in mid-2002. He injured his shoulder while fielding in a tour match in which he started well with a total of 5/70, and was forced to miss the First Test in Guyana.After taking only six wickets at 38 upon his return to the team for the Second and Third Tests, he was dropped for the Fourth Test, but was recalled again for the Fifth Test at Sabina Park, after Kumble was injured. Despite taking improved match figures of 8/180, including 5/138 in the first innings, Harbhajan was unable to prevent an Indian defeat after the batting collapsed in the first innings.He claimed three wickets in the three match ODI series at 33.00, conceding 4.71 runs per over.

Despite his performance at Sabina Park, Harbhajan was dropped again when Kumble returned for the First Test on the tour to England at Lord's, where the hosts prevailed. India's coach John Wright later admitted that Harbhajan's omission had been a mistake. Harbhajan returned for the final three Tests with moderate success, taking 12 wickets at 34.16, improving as the English summer wore on. After claiming 3/175 in the drawn Second Test, he struck form in the tour match against Essex, taking 7/83 and 1/ 23. He then took 3/40 and 1/56 as India levelled the series in the Third Test at Headingley, before taking 5/115 in the first innings of the Fourth Test at The Oval, as well as managing his second Test half-century of 54 at Trent Bridge in the Second Test.He ended the series with 90 runs at 22.50.

for the entire tour, Harbhajan aggregated 28 wickets at 27.60. Harbhajan had modest results in the Natwest Trophy. After being dropped after one wicketless match, he was dropped and then took 4/46 against Sri Lanka in the last match before the final to ensure his retention, but went wicketless in the decider, which India won. He played in three ODIs and took four wickets at 37.25 at 4.96.

- *2002 Champions Trophy*

The 2002 ICC Champions Trophy in Sri Lanka at the end of the tour brought moderate results with six wickets at 30.66 at an economy rate of only 3.68, and a best of 3/27 from ten overs in the firstwashed out final against the host nation. Harbhajan helped restrict Sri Lanka to 5/244, but rain ended proceedings with India at 0/14. He then took 1/34 the next day during a replay of the final. This time the hosts made 7/222 and a downpour again thwarted the players, with India at 1/38 when play was called off and the trophy shared.

As was the case in the previous season, Harbhajan's return to Indian soil coincided with an improvement in results. He took 1/37 and 7/48 in an innings victory at Mumbai in the First Test against the West Indies, and then contributed match figures of 3/56, 4/ 79 and 37 in an eight-wicket victory in Chennai which saw him named man of the match. A haul of 5/115 in the Third Test at Calcutta was the best in a high scoring match, and with 20 wickets at 16.75 and 69 runs at 17.25, Harbhajan was named as the man of the series. He was unable to transfer his performances to the ODI format, taking only five wickets at 49.00 against the same team at an economy rate of 5.44. Harbhajan took only five wickets at 18.80 in the subsequent Test tour to New Zealand, in a series where five pace bowlers averaged less than 20 on green, seaming tracks. India lost the series 2–0 and Harbhajan's 20 and 18 in the Second Test amounted for more than 15% of India's match total.The off spinner then took 1/56 in one ODI before heading for his World Cup debut in South Africa.

- *2003 World Cup*

Harbhajan had a mixed tournament at the 2003 Cricket World Cup, taking 11 wickets at 30.45 with an economy rate of 3.92 in ten matches. He was the first-choice spinner and played in all matches but one, being dropped for the victory against arch-rivals Pakistan in the group phase. His counterpart, Kumble, played in only three matches.

Harbhajan was steady throughout the tournament, never taking more than two wickets in a match, and never conceding more than 42 runs from his quota of ten overs, except in the two matches against Australia, who went through the tournament without defeat. In the group match, Harbhajan was the second highest score, with a counter-attacking 28 as India collapsed for 125, but when it was his turn to bowl, the Australians attacked him and scored 49 runs from his 44 balls without losing a wicket in a decisive nine-wicket win. In the final, Ganguly elected to field and Harbhajan was the only Indian bowler to take a wicket, taking 2/49 from eight overs. In contrast, the Australians scored at 7.38 runs per over from the other bowlers to reach 2/359.

the highest total in a World Cup final, and win by 125 runs. He was the fourth leading wicket taker for India overall and his tournament bowling average was worse than those of Zaheer Khan, Ashish Nehra and Javagal Srinath. He finished the season with six wickets at 14.00 at 3.65 runs per over in three matches in an ODI tournament in Bangladesh, where he was fined for abusing an umpire.

- *Finger injury*

After experiencing pains in his spinning finger during the World Cup, Harbhajan was scheduled to undergo surgery in mid-2003 in Australia, but the surgery was delayed as he sought to play through the pain. He underwent physiotherapy in lieu of surgery and was declared fit for a two-match Test series at home against New Zealand in late 2003. His performance was substantially worse than his previous displays on Indian soil, taking only six wickets at an average of 50.00 as both matches ended in high-scoring draws. Aside from his debut series, it was his worst series bowling average on Indian soil.

Despite a triangular ODI series against New Zealand and Australia in which he managed only four wickets at 40.50 in four matches and spent time in the sidelines, the Indian team attempted to manage his injury rather than have his finger operated on, and took him on the 2003–04 tour of Australia. As with his previous visit four years earlier, Harbhajan had an unhappy time, taking 2/159 in a tour match against Victoria.After an ineffective 1/169 in the First Test at Brisbane, his injury deteriorated and he underwent major finger surgery, sidelining him for a predicted five months. Kumble replaced him and took 24 wickets in the remaining three Tests in strak contrast of Harbhajan's struggles in Australia. Kumble bowled India to victory in the following Test against Pakistan in Multan, taking 6/71 to reclaim his position as the No. 1 spinner.

After a seven-month layoff, Harbhajan returned to represent India in ODIs in the Asia Cup in July 2004, where he took four wickets at 39.75 in four matches at 3.97 runs per over. His performance improved on the tour to England for an ODI series against England and the 2004 ICC Champions Trophy, taking eight wickets at 14.00, conceding only 2.80 runs an over, including 3/28 against England and 3/33 against Kenya and hitting as an unbeaten 41 against England at The Oval as India's batting collapsed to a substantial defeat.

Harbhajan made his Test return against Australia, who were again seeking their first series win on Indian soil since 1969 in the late 2004 home series. Harbhajan took 5/146 in the first innings and 6/78 in the second innings in addition to making a run out to reduce Australia from 103/3 to 228 all out. Despite this, India required 457 in their second innings to win, slumping to 125/8 before Harbhajan (42) and Irfan Pathan helped India to reach 239 after a rearguard counter-attack, still a 217-run loss.

Harbhajan was less effective in the drawn Second Test in Chennai, with match figures of 5/198, which was washed out with India still needing 210 more runs on the last day with all ten wickets in hand.Harbhajan then withdrew from the Third Test in Nagpur due to illness.Australia won the match easily, clinching the series. Harbhajan returned for the final Test in Mumbai. After failing to take a wicket in the first innings, he claimed 5/29 in the second to help India bowl Australia out for 93 and claim a dramatic 14-run victory. Harbhajan ended the series with 21 wickets at 24.00 and 69 runs at 13.80.

A Test series in India against South Africa followed, with Harbhajan taking match figures of 4/166 in the drawn First Test in Kanpur, before producing a man of the match performance in the Second Test in Calcutta to lead India to a 1–0 series win. After taking 2/54 in the first innings, he took 6/78 in the second, including South Africa's first five batsman to help dismiss the tourists for 222. This set up a run-chase of 117, which India reached with eight wickets in hand.

Harbhajan was the leading wicket-taker for the series, with 13 victims at an average of 23.61. He ended 2004 with a quiet tour of Bangladesh, scoring a 47 in the Second Test and taking four wickets at 41.75 in two Tests and one wicket at 94 at an economy rate of 5.22 in two ODIs.He had a relatively light workload, bowling only 47.4 overs in the Tests, as Irfan Pathan frequently scythed through the Bangladeshi batsmen with the new ball, taking three five wicket hauls. He then returned to India and took a total of 6/172 in North Zone's seven-wicket win over South.

His performance in Bangladesh saw him dropped for the First Test in the early 2005 series against Pakistan on his home ground in Mohali, with Kumble being the only spinner selected on the pace-friendly surface.India were in control of the match for four days, and needed only four wickets on day five, but were unable to break the Pakistani lower-order until play was almost over and the tourists had taken a lead, and the match ended in a draw.

Harbhajan was recalled for the Second Test in Calcutta and took match figures of 4/145 in an Indian victory. Despite taking 6/152 in a marathon 51-over spell in the first innings of the Third Test in Bangalore, Pakistan won the match to level the series after India collapsed on the final day. Harbhajan finished the series with 10 wickets at 33.20. His performance in the subsequent ODI series was even worse, managing only three wickets at 73.66 in five matches at an economy rate of 4.80. In spite of the poor end to the season, his performance in the year since finger surgery in the long form of the game saw him nominated for the 2005 ICC Test Player of the Year.

Harbhajan spent the international off-season playing for Surrey in English county cricket, citing the improvement that other international players had gained from such an experience. It was his first stint in county cricket, after a planned season at Lancashire in 2003 was cancelled due to injury. After taking six wickets in his opening two first-class fixtures, he struck form against Hampshire, taking 6/36 and 2/47 in an innings triumph. In is fourth and final first-class match, against Gloucestershire, Harbhajan took a total of 6/193 and equalled his previous first-class best of 84. He ended with 20 wickets at 25.85 and 124 runs at 31.00. In the Twenty20 competition, he had less success in the new format, taking four wickets at 38.00 at an economy rate of 6.60 in eight matches. In all he spent six weeks with the county.

- *Test decline*

- Harbhajan Singh arrives at training.

2006 began with Harbhajan's first tour to arch-rivals Pakistan. The First Test was a high scoring draw held in Lahore, where Harbhajan recorded his worst ever Test figures of 0/176, conceding more than five runs an over in a match where 1,089 runs were scored for the loss of just eight wickets. In a match in which many batting records fell, Harbhajan was hit for 27 runs in one over by Shahid Afridi, just one short of the world record.The second Test in Faisalabad was another high scoring draw, with the aggregate runs being the fourth highest in Test history. Harbhajan took 0/101 and 0/78. His 81 overs in the series were the fourth highest number of overs in any Test series without taking a wicket.When he was given the opportunity to make use of the batting surface in India's only innings in Faisalabad, he managed a brisk 38, including two sixes. Harbhajan was dropped for the Third Test in Karachi, where a green pitch promised to favour seam bowling, and Kumble was the only spinner used. After sustaining an injury, Harbhajan was sent home during the subsequent ODI series without playing a match, ending his tour without taking a wicket.

- Harbhajan with India in 2006

A return to Indian soil for the Test series against England failed to ease Harbhajan's wicket-taking difficulties. He managed match figures of 2/172 in the drawn First Test in Nagpur, and 1/83 in the Second Test in Mohali, where his main contribution was to hit 36 runs, helping India to a first innings lead. Despite taking 3/89 and 2/40 in the Third Test in Mumbai, Harbhajan ended the series with eight wickets at an average of 48.00, nearly twice his career average on Indian soil.

Despite his difficulties in Test cricket, Harbhajan's ODI form remained strong, as he top-scored with a rearguard 37 out of 203 and then took 5/31 in a man of the match performance in the first ODI against England in Delhi, sparking a collapse of 7/47 which secured a 39-run victory.He ended the series with 12 wickets at 15.58 at an economy rate of 3.74 from five matches, and topped the wicket-taking list despite being rested for the last match, as well as having the best bowling average and economy rate.India took the series 5–1, Harbhajan taking 3/30 in their only loss.

Harbhajan was unable to maintain his ODI form on the tour to the West Indies, where he managed three wickets at 64 in five matches, although he continued to be economical, conceding 3.91 runs per over. He was omitted from the Test team for the opening two Tests as India opted to use three pace bowlers and Anil Kumble, scrapping the five bowler strategy used since early 2006. The reasons for the return to the four-man attack were unclear, with performance, fatigue and injury variously offered as explanations. Harbhajan was recalled for the Third Test in St Kitts after the pace attack was unable to dismiss the West Indian batsmen, with local captain Brian Lara stating that his team, who had three wickets in hand at the end of play, would have been lucky to draw the Second Test had Harbhajan been playing. In a drawn match, Harbhajan claimed the leading match figures of 6/186, as well as contributing an unbeaten 38 in the first innings.

Harbhajan's 5/13 in 27 balls in the first innings in the Fourth Test saw the hosts lose their last six wickets for 23, to give India a 97 run first innings lead. India went on secure a victory in a low scoring match in three days and win the series 1–0, although Harbhajan was punished in the second innings, conceding 65 runs in 16 overs without taking a wicket. It was India's first series victory in the Caribbean in 35 years, with Harbhajan contributing 11 wickets at 24.00.

The 2006–07 season began with the DLF Cup in Malaysia, where Harbhajan made a good start to the season, taking six wickets at 19.16 at an economy rate of 3.59 in four matches. He was man of the match against the West Indies, scoring 37 in a 78-run partnership to push India to 162, before taking 3/35 to secure a 16-run victory. India failed to reach the final, contested by Australia and the West Indies. Harbhajan was unable to maintain his form in the 2006 ICC Champions Trophy held in India, managing only two wickets at 51.50 and saving his worst performance of 0/49 in the final group match against Australia on his home ground in Punjab.

India won only one of their three matches and were eliminated, although Harbhajan continued to be tidy, conceding 3.67 runs per over. The tour of South Africa in late 2006 saw even less success, taking only one wicket in three ODI matches while conceding 161 runs at the expensive economy rate of 5.75. He finished the year watching from the sidelines as India fielded Kumble as the only spinner in the three Test series, which India lost 2–1. Apart from the injury hit 2003, it was Harbhajan's least productive year in Test cricket since he became a regular team member in 2001, managing only 19 wickets at 52.78.

Harbhajan returned for the early 2007 ODI series against the West Indies and Sri Lanka in India, taking seven wickets at 36.00 in seven matches at an economy rate of 4.27. Despite criticism that he was afraid to toss the ball up, and was concentrating on bowling flat in a defensive run-saving style, Harbhajan was selected as the off spin bowler in the Indian squad for the 2007 Cricket World Cup, while Ramesh Powar, who had been more expensive but had taken more wickets in recent times, was omitted.A statistical study showed that since the start of 2006, Harbhajan has been the second most economical bowler in the final 10 overs of ODIs.

During the 2007 Cricket World Cup, Harbhajan started as India's first-choice spinner and played in their first match against Bangladesh. He took 0/30 from his ten overs, but India lost the match as their batsmen collapsed and Bangladesh had no need to take risks against the bowling. Harbhajan was dropped in favour of Kumble for the second match against Bermuda, which India won easily. Harbhajan was recalled for the final group match against Sri Lanka, and had little effect, taking 0/53 from his ten overs as India were set 255 for victory. Harbhajan made an unbeaten 17 as India collapsed to 185 to lose the match and be eliminated in the group phase.

Following the failed campaign, the Indian selectors made multiple changes to the national team and Harbhajan was dropped for the tours of Bangladesh and England. Rajesh Pawar, Piyush Chawla and Powar were the spinners selected to partner Kumble.Harbhajan's waning wicket-taking and his lack of flight were again perceived to be the cause of his problems.

In the meantime, Harbhajan played in two ODIs for the Asian Cricket Council against a combined African team, taking 1/53 and 3/48 as the Asians won both matches. He then returned to Surrey for a second season of county cricket in an attempt to rediscover his form while his compatriots were touring England, staying throughout July and August. After easing into the season with six wickets in the first two first-class matches, Harbhajan found a rich vein of form, taking 4/64 and 5/64 against Worcestershire, before following up with 5/34 and 6/57 against Kent, finishing off by scoring 29 to help guide Surrey home by four wickets after they had stumbled in pursuit of 107. He ended the first-class campaign with five and six wickets against Durham and Hampshire respectively and totalled 37 wickets at 18.54 in only six outings. He was not so successful in the one-dayers, taking six wickets at 29.50 and an economy rate of 4.65 in five matches.

- *Revival*

Harbhajan returned to international cricket for the tour of Sri Lanka in July and August. In the First Test at Colombo, he took 2/149 as Sri Lanka amassed 600/6 declared and won by an innings. In the Second Test in Galle, he took 6/102 to help India take a first innings lead of 37 and then took 4/51 in the second innings to help India level the series with a 170-run win. It was his fifth ten-wicket match haul and his first outside India. He was again India's leading wicket-taker in the Third Test defeat, with 3/104 and 1/44. He was India's leading wicket-taker with 16 scalps at 28.12, twice as many the second most-prolific Indian.In the subsequent ODI series, he played in the first four matches, taking six wickets at 18.83 at an economy rate of 3.80, including 3/40 in the win in the fourth match, which sealed the series. He was rested from the final dead rubber.

At the start of the Indian season, Harbhajan took 2/32 and 4/ 31 as the Rest of India defeated Delhi in the Irani Trophy. This was followed by the First Test against Australia in Bangalore. Harbhajan took Ponting's wicket in taking 1/103 in the first innings, but not before the Australian captain had scored 123. In reply to Australia's 430, India were in trouble at 195/6 when Harbhajan came in to bat. He scored a rearguard 54, putting on 80 with fellow bowler Zaheer Khan, to reduce India's deficit to 70. He then took 2/76 in the second innings as the match ended in a draw. Ponting later cited Harbhajan and Zaheer's partnership as the passage of play that prevented an Australian win. In the Second Test at his home ground in Mohali, Harbhajan took 2/60 in the first innings as India took a 201-run first innings lead.

In the second innings Australia were chasing 516 for victory and had started aggressively, reaching 49/0 after seven overs. Harbhajan was introduced into the attack and removed Hayden and Simon Katich in his first over and then Mike Hussey in his next.

This triggered Australia's collapse to 58/5 and their eventual defeat by 320 runs. Harbhajan was unable to find a fourth wicket, which would have seen him reach 300 Test wickets on his home ground, and ended with 3/36. He was then ruled out of the drawn Third Test because of a toe injury.

Harbhajan returned for the Fourth Test in Nagpur and dismissed Ponting for the tenth time in Tests in the first innings to register his 300th wicket. He ended with 3/94 as India took an 86-run lead. However, a batting collapse meant that India were 6/166 at tea on day four, only 252 runs ahead and facing possible defeat if Australia could clean up the tail quickly. Harbhajan then scored 52, combining in a 107-run partnership with captain Mahendra Singh Dhoni to guide India out of trouble. India then successfully defended the target of 380 to win by 172 runs, with Harbhajan taking 4/64 including top-scorer Hayden and the final wicket.

Harbhajan was the equal-leading wicket-taker for the series along with Ishant Sharma, taking 15 wickets at 28.86. He also scored 125 runs at 41.66, helping to prevent two defeats. The series also saw the end of Harbhajan's partnership with Kumble, who missed the Second Test due to injury and then retired after suffering another wound in the next match. As a result, Harbhajan started a new pairing with leg spinner Amit Mishra.

In the five-match home ODI series against England, Harbhajan took seven wickets at 30.29 and an economy rate of 5.04 as India won 5–0. He took one wicket in each of the matches, except the third match in Kanpur. In that match, he took 3/31, registered his 200th ODI wicket and was named man-of-the match. During the two Tests, Harbhajan was the equal-leading wicket-taker with eight wickets at 35.00 and he also scored 69 runs at 34.50.This included a 40 in the first innings of the First Test to help India reach 241 after a top-order collapse, keeping India's deficit to 75; they went on to win the match. Harbhajan ended the year as the third-highest wicket-taker in the world, and the highest among Indian players. He was named by Wisden in their selection of the Test team of the year.

- *2009 ICC tournaments*

Harbhajan was part of the Indian team that attempted to defend their crown at the 2009 World Twenty20. However they lost all three of their matches in the Super 8s round and were eliminated. Harbhajan took 3/30 in one of those matches against England, and ended the tournament with five wickets at 26.20 and an economy rate of 6.55. During the tour of the West Indies that followed, Harbhajan took three wickets at 45.33, conceding almost a run a ball in three ODIs as India prevailed 2–1.

In September, Harbhajan took 5/56 in the final of the Compaq Cup to help secure a 46-run Indian win over the hosts Sri Lanka. It was his first five-wicket haul in three years and capped off a tournament in which he took six wickets at 22.00 in three matches. He then struggled at the 2009 ICC Champions Trophy in South Africa, taking 1/71 from ten overs against Pakistan and 0/54 from nine overs against Australia. India lost to Pakistan and the latter match was washed out. He then took 2/14 from eight overs against the West Indies, but it was not enough to prevent India from being eliminated in the first round, despite winning the match.

Harbhajan bowling during India's two-match Test series against Australia in October 2010

- *2010 season*

After his travails in South Africa, Harbhajan started the Indian season with eight wickets at 12.87 in three Challenger Trophy one-dayers for India Blue. He then played in a home ODI series against Australia taking eight wickets at 33.87 at an economy rate of 4.51 in six games. This included a best of 2/23 in the sixth match, but he made a more influential contribution in the first match with the bat, striking 49 at the death as India came within striking distance of their target before he fell in the last over and the hosts ended five runs adrift of the target. He scored a similarly rapid 31 in the fourth match, but India fell 24 runs short. Harbhajan ended the series with

81 runs at 20.25.

In the three home Tests against Sri Lanka, Harbhajan was the highest wicket-taker with 13 scalps, but these came at an average cost of 41.00. After taking 2/189 in the drawn First Test, he aggregated 5/152 and 6/192 as India took the next two fixtures by an innings. In the subsequent ODI series, he took six wickets at 35.00 at an economy rate of 4.88 as India won 3–1. He took 2/58 from his ten overs in the first match, which proved to be tidy in the context of a match in which both teams passed 410 and India prevailed by three runs.

During the tri-series in Bangladesh in January 2010, Harbhajan took six wickets at 24.00 in three matches. He missed the First Test due to neck pain but returned to take a total of 2/123 as India completed a clean sweep with a ten-wicket win in the Second Test.

During New Zealand's tour of India in November 2010, Harbhajan scored his maiden Test century during the First Test in Ahmedabad. This was the 100th century by an Indian in the second innings and he reached triple figures with a six. His 115, along with Laxman's 91 saved the game for India after they had collapsed to 5/15. Harbhajan was named man of the match. He followed on in the next test with 111* in India's 1st innings, becoming the first no. 8 batsman to score back-to-back test centuries.

After an ordinary performance with the ball in the 5-match ODI series in West Indies in June 2011 (where he was the vice captain to skipper Suresh Raina) (took 4 wickets from 3 matches, best of 3/32), he helped his team revive from dire straits in the 1st Test in Sabina Park at Kingston, Jamaica. With India struggling at 85/6, he along with Suresh Raina initiated a counter-attack to string an aggressive 146-run partnership with Suresh Raina(82 off 115 balls, 15 fours) to help India reach 246. Harbhajan scored 70 from 74 balls (10 fours, 1 six).

- *2017 Champions Trophy exclusion*

Harbhajan was again excluded from the Indian squad for the 2017 Champions Trophy in England. After hearing of his exclusion, Harbhajan claimed he did not receive the same "privileges" other veteran cricketers, namely MS Dhoni, have been afforded by the national selectors. After the media pounced on this comment, Harbhajan claimed the media frenzy took his statement out of proportion.

- *1998 suspension*

Harbhajan was fined and given a suspended ban for one ODI by the match referee in his first international series, when his on-field behaviour was adjudged to breach the ICC Code of Conduct. The incident in question was his altercation with Ricky Ponting after dismissing him.

- *Altercations with Andrew Symonds and Sreesanth*

While Harbhajan was batting during his 63 on the third day of the Second Test at the Sydney Cricket Ground, he became involved in an altercation with Australia's Andrew Symonds. As a result of this, he was charged with a Level 3 offence of racially abusing Symonds by calling the Australian—of Caribbean descent—a "monkey". Harbhajan and Tendulkar, his batting partner at the time of the incident, denied this.At a hearing after the conclusion of the Test, match referee Mike Procter found Harbhajan guilty and banned him for three Tests. This decision generated controversy because no audio or video evidence was available, and the conviction relied on the testimony of the Australian players. The Indian team initially threatened to withdraw from the series pending an appeal against Harbhajan's suspension, however BCCI president Sharad Pawar later claimed that the tour would proceed even if the second hearing was unsuccessful.

Harbhajan (left), batting with Tendulkar during the Second Test at the SCG. The altercation with Symonds occurred during their partnership.

On 29 January, following the Fourth Test, the appeal hearing was conducted in Adelaide by ICC Appeals Commissioner Justice John Hansen. The result was that the racism charge was not proved, resulting in the revocation of the three-Test ban imposed by Procter. However, Harbhajan was found guilty of using abusive language and fined 50% of his match fee. Hansen later admitted he "could have imposed a more serious penalty if he was made aware by the ICC of the bowler's previous transgressions"—including a suspended one-Test ban. It was reported that senior players from both sides had written a letter to Hansen requesting that the charge be downgraded. According to this report, the letter was signed by Tendulkar and Ponting and counter-signed by Michael Clarke, Hayden and Symonds.

In the aftermath of the hearing, Hayden called Harbhajan an "obnoxious weed" during a radio interview, which earned him a code of conduct violation charge from Cricket Australia.

Harbhajan was involved in further controversy after an 2008 Indian Premier League (IPL) match between Mumbai Indians and Kings XI Punjab at Mohali in April 2008. While the teams were shaking hands, he slapped Kerala paceman and Indian teammate Sreesanth in the face.

Harbhajan, who had stood in as the Mumbai captain for the first three matches of the tournament to that point, all of which were lost, had apparently been angered by Sreesanth's aggressive sending-off of his batsmen as Punjab coasted to a decisive victory. The Kings XI Punjab lodged an official complaint to the IPL. The match referee Farokh Engineer found Harbhajan guilty of a level 4.2 offence, banning him from the remainder of the IPL and preventing him from claiming his entire season's salary.

Harbhajan made up with Sreesanth, and said that "I have been punished for the wrong I did". Harbhajan had taken five wickets at 16.40 at an economy rate of 8.20 and scored 30 runs at 15.00 in the three matches before his ban. On 14 May, the BCCI disciplinary committee found Harbhajan guilty under Rule 3.2.1 of their regulations and handed down the maximum punishment of five-match ban from ODIs. Harbhajan faces the prospect of a life ban if he commits significant disciplinary breaches in the future.

As a result, Harbhajan missed the tri-series in Bangladesh and the 2008 Asia Cup in Pakistan, and India went down in the final of both tournaments after qualifying first on both occasions. He would have been eligible for selection after the first two matches of the Asia Cup, but the selectors omitted him entirely.

In 2021, tendered an unconditional apology for sharing a social media post with a picture of Khalistani militant Jarnail Singh Bhindranwale to pay homage to those who died in 'Operation Bluestar' of 1984. Facing backlash from all quarters, Harbhajan said he posted a WhatsApp forward on the 37th anniversary of the operation without realizing that the man in the picture was Bhindranwale.

- Twitter fight with Mohammad Amir

On 27 October 2021, Harbhajan Singh was involved in ugly spat with Pakistani cricketer Mohammad Amir on Twitter following India's lost to Pakistan in 2021 ICC Men's T20 World Cup.

- *Playing style*

Harbhajan is an attacking-minded bowler who is regarded for his ball control and ability to vary his length and pace, although he is often criticised for his flat trajectory.His main wicket-taking ball climbs wickedly on the unsuspecting batsman from a good length, forcing him to alter his stroke at the last second.With a whippy bowling action, he was reported for throwing in November 1998. Although forced to travel to England for tests, his action was cleared by former English player Fred Titmus.

He has developed an ability to bowl the doosra, which was the subject of an official report by match referee Chris Broad, on-field umpires Aleem Dar and Mark Benson, and TV umpire Mahbubur

Rahman after the Second Test between India and Bangladesh at Chittagong, Bangladesh in December 2004. The ICC cleared his action in May 2005, saying that the straightening of his elbow fell within the permitted limits.

Among off spinners, Harbhajan is the second highest wicket-taker in Test history, behind Muttiah Muralitharan of Sri Lanka. He is the third-highest Test wicket-taker among all Indians.Harbhajan average with the ball in home Test matches hovers in the mid-20s. All five of his man of the match awards and both of his man of the series awards have been obtained in India.Outside India, his bowling average climbs to around 40. Statistically, his bowling in Test matches is most effective against the West Indies and Australia.

As of May 2008, his most productive hunting grounds have been Eden Gardens in Calcutta, where he has taken 38 wickets at 23.10 in six Tests, while the Chepauk in Chennai, where he has claimed two-man of the match awards, has yield 34 wickets at 24.25 in five Tests. Harbhajan has claimed his wickets most cheaply at Wankhede Stadium in Mumbai, where he has taken 22 wickets at 19.45. Compared to Muralitharan, Harbhajan is less reliant on targeting the stumps for his dismissals; he captures more than 60% of his wickets via catches and less than 25% by bowling or trapping batsmen leg before wicket, whereas the corresponding figures for Muralitharan are in the 40s.

Harbhajan's off spin complements Kumble's leg spin. While Harbhajan is known for his emotional and extroverted celebrations, which are part of a deliberate strategy of aggression, Kumble is known for his undemonstrative and composed approach.Both spinners have opined that they bowl more effectively in tandem via persistent application of pressure to batsmen, but statistics have shown that while Kumble has performed better when paired with Harbhajan, Harbhajan has been more effective in Kumble's absence.

In an interview in 2001, Harbhajan stated his ambition to become an all-rounder. Although he has recorded a few half-centuries at Test level, his batting average hovers around 15 in both Tests and ODIs. However, in the span of four years starting from 2003, he has shown improved performance, averaging around 20 with the bat. His style is frequently described as unorthodox, with pundits agreeing with his self-assessment attributing his batting achievements to his hand-eye coordination, rather than his footwork or technique. The aggression in Harbhajan's bowling also extends to his batting, with a Test strike rate in the 60s, placing him in the ten highest strike rates among players who have scored more than 1000 runs in Test cricket.

CHAPTER TWO

Let's Know About Cricket

- *Cricket*

Cricket is a bat-and-ball game played between two teams of eleven players on a field at the centre of which is a 22-yard (20-metre) pitch with a wicket at each end, each comprising two bails balanced on three stumps. The game proceeds when a player on the fielding team, called the bowler, "bowls" (propels) the ball from one end of the pitch towards the wicket at the other end. The batting side's players score runs by striking the bowled ball with a bat and running between the wickets, while the bowling side tries to prevent this by keeping the ball within the field and getting it to either wicket, and dismiss each batter (so they are "out"). Means of dismissal include being bowled, when the ball hits the stumps and dislodges the bails, and by the fielding side either catching a hit ball before it touches the ground, or hitting a wicket with the ball before a batter can cross the crease line in front of the wicket to complete a run. When ten batters have been dismissed, the innings ends and the teams swap roles. The game is adjudicated by two umpires, aided by a third umpire and match referee in international matches.

Forms of cricket range from Twenty20, with each team batting for a single innings of 20 overs and the game generally lasting three hours, to Test matches played over five days. Traditionally cricketers play in all-white kit, but in limited overs cricket they wear club or team colours. In addition to the basic kit, some players wear protective gear to prevent injury caused by the ball, which is a hard, solid spheroid made of compressed leather with a slightly raised sewn seam enclosing a cork core layered with tightly wound string.

The earliest reference to cricket is in South East England in the mid-16th century. It spread globally with the expansion of the British Empire, with the first international matches in the second half of the 19th century. The game's governing body is the International Cricket Council (ICC), which has over 100 members, twelve of which are full members who play Test matches. The game's rules, the Laws of Cricket, are maintained by Marylebone Cricket Club (MCC) in London. The sport is followed primarily in South Asia, Australasia, the United Kingdom, southern Africa and the West Indies.Women's cricket, which is organised and played separately, has also achieved international standard. The most successful side playing international cricket is Australia, which has won seven One Day International trophies, including five World Cups, more than any other country and has been the top-rated Test side more than any other country.

- *History of cricket to 1725*

A medieval "club ball" game involving an underhand bowl towards a batter. Ball catchers are shown positioning themselves to catch a ball. Detail from the Canticles of Holy Mary, 13th century.

Cricket is one of many games in the "club ball" sphere that basically involve hitting a ball with a hand-held implement; others include baseball (which shares many similarities with cricket, both belonging in the more specific bat-and-ball games category), golf, hockey, tennis, squash, badminton and table tennis. In cricket's case, a key difference is the existence of a solid target structure, the wicket (originally, it is thought, a "wicket gate" through which sheep were herded), that the batter must defend. The cricket historian Harry Altham identified three "groups" of "club ball" games: the "hockey group", in which the ball is driven to and fro between two targets (the goals); the "golf group", in which the ball is driven towards an undefended target (the hole); and the "cricket group", in which "the ball is aimed at a mark (the wicket) and driven away from it".

It is generally believed that cricket originated as a children's game in the south-eastern counties of England, sometime during the medieval period.Although there are claims for prior dates, the earliest definite reference to cricket being played comes from evidence given at a court case in Guildford in January 1597 (Old Style), equating to January 1598 in the modern calendar. The case concerned ownership of a certain plot of land and the court heard the testimony of a 59-year-old coroner, John Derrick, who gave witness that.

Being a scholler in the ffree schoole of Guldeford hee and diverse of his fellows did runne and play there at creckett and other plaies.

Given Derrick's age, it was about half a century earlier when he was at school and so it is certain that cricket was being played c. 1550 by boys in Surrey. The view that it was originally a children's game is reinforced by Randle Cotgrave's 1611 English-French dictionary in which he defined the noun "crosse" as "the crooked staff wherewith boys play at cricket" and the verb form "crosser" as "to play at cricket".

One possible source for the sport's name is the Old English word "cryce" (or "cricc") meaning a crutch or staff. In Samuel Johnson's Dictionary, he derived cricket from "cryce, Saxon, a stick". In Old French, the word "criquet" seems to have meant a kind of club or stick. Given the strong medieval trade connections between south-east England and the County of Flanders when the latter belonged to the Duchy of Burgundy, the name may have been derived from the Middle Dutch (in use in Flanders at the time) "krick"(-e), meaning a stick (crook). Another possible source is the Middle Dutch word "krickstoel", meaning a long low stool used for kneeling in church and which resembled the long low wicket with two stumps used in early cricket. According to Heiner Gillmeister, a European language expert of Bonn University, "cricket" derives from the Middle Dutch phrase for hockey, met de (krik ket)sen (i.e., "with the stick chase"). Gillmeister has suggested that not only the name but also the sport itself may be of Flemish origin.

- Growth of amateur and professional cricket in England

Evolution of the cricket bat. The original "hockey stick" (left) evolved into the straight bat from c. 1760 when pitched delivery bowling began.

Although the main object of the game has always been to score the most runs, the early form of cricket differed from the modern game in certain key technical aspects; the North American variant of cricket known as wicket retained many of these aspects. The ball was bowled underarm by the bowler and along the ground towards a batter armed with a bat that in shape resembled a hockey stick; the batter defended a low, two-stump wicket; and runs were called notches because the scorers recorded them by notching tally sticks.

In 1611, the year Cotgrave's dictionary was published, ecclesiastical court records at Sidlesham in Sussex state that two parishioners, Bartholomew Wyatt and Richard Latter, failed to attend church on Easter Sunday because they were playing cricket. They were fined 12d each and ordered to do penance.This is the earliest mention of adult participation in cricket and it was around the same time that the earliest known organised inter-parish or village match was played – at Chevening, Kent. In 1624, a player called Jasper Vinall died after he was accidentally struck on the head during a match between two parish teams in Sussex.

Cricket remained a low-key local pursuit for much of the 17th century. It is known, through numerous references found in the records of ecclesiastical court cases, to have been proscribed at times by the Puritans before and during the Commonwealth. The problem was nearly always the issue of Sunday play as the Puritans considered cricket to be "profane" if played on the Sabbath, especially if large crowds or gambling were involved.

According to the social historian Derek Birley, there was a "great upsurge of sport after the Restoration" in 1660. Gambling on sport became a problem significant enough for Parliament to pass the 1664 Gambling Act, limiting stakes to £100 which was, in any case, a colossal sum exceeding the annual income of 99% of the population. Along with prizefighting, horse racing and blood sports, cricket was perceived to be a gambling sport.Rich patrons made matches for high stakes, forming teams in which they engaged the first professional players.By the end of the century, cricket had developed into a major sport that was spreading throughout England and was already being taken abroad by English mariners and colonisers – the earliest reference to cricket overseas is dated 1676. A 1697 newspaper report survives of "a great cricket match" played in Sussex "for fifty guineas apiece" – this is the earliest known contest that is generally considered a First Class match.

- The patrons, and other players from the social class known as the "gentry", began to classify themselves as "amateurs"[fn 1] to establish a clear distinction from the professionals, who were invariably members of the working class, even to the point of having separate changing and dining facilities. The gentry, including such high-ranking nobles as the Dukes of Richmond, exerted their honour code of noblesse oblige to claim rights of leadership in any sporting contests they took part in, especially as it was necessary for them to play alongside their "social inferiors" if they were to win their bets. In time, a perception took hold that the typical amateur who played in first-class cricket, until 1962 when amateurism was abolished, was someone with a public school education who had then gone to one of Cambridge or Oxford University – society insisted that such people were "officers and gentlemen" whose destiny was to provide leadership. In a purely financial sense, the cricketing amateur would theoretically claim expenses for playing while his professional counterpart played under contract and was paid a wage or match fee; in practice, many amateurs claimed more than actual expenditure and the derisive term "shamateur" was coined to describe the practice.

- The Young Cricketer, 1768

The game underwent major development in the 18th century to become England's national sport.Its success was underwritten by the twin necessities of patronage and betting. Cricket was prominent in London as early as 1707 and, in the middle years of the century, large crowds flocked to matches on the Artillery Ground in Finsbury. The single wicket form of the sport attracted huge crowds and wagers to match, its popularity peaking in the 1748 season. Bowling underwent an evolution around 1760 when bowlers began to pitch the ball instead of rolling or skimming it towards the batter. This caused a revolution in bat design because, to deal with the bouncing ball, it was necessary to introduce the modern straight bat in place of the old "hockey stick" shape.

The Hambledon Club was founded in the 1760s and, for the next twenty years until the formation of Marylebone Cricket Club (MCC) and the opening of Lord's Old Ground in 1787, Hambledon was both the game's greatest club and its focal point. MCC quickly became the sport's premier club and the custodian of the Laws of Cricket. New Laws introduced in the latter part of the 18th century included the three stump wicket and leg before wicket (lbw).

The 19th century saw underarm bowling superseded by first roundarm and then overarm bowling. Both developments were controversial.Organisation of the game at county level led to the creation of the county clubs, starting with Sussex in 1839. In December 1889, the eight leading county clubs formed the official County Championship, which began in 1890.

The most famous player of the 19th century was W. G. Grace, who started his long and influential career in 1865. It was especially during the career of Grace that the distinction between amateurs and professionals became blurred by the existence of players like him who were nominally amateur but, in terms of their financial gain, de facto professional. Grace himself was said to have been paid more money for playing cricket than any professional.

The last two decades before the First World War have been called the "Golden Age of cricket". It is a nostalgic name prompted by the collective sense of loss resulting from the war, but the period did produce some great players and memorable matches, especially as organised competition at county and Test level developed.

- Cricket becomes an international sport

In 1844, the first-ever international match took place between the United States and Canada. In 1859, a team of English players went to North America on the first overseas tour. Meanwhile, the British Empire had been instrumental in spreading the game overseas and by the middle of the 19th century it had become well established in Australia, the Caribbean, India, Pakistan, New Zealand, North America and South Africa.

In 1862, an English team made the first tour of Australia. The first Australian team to travel overseas consisted of Aboriginal stockmen who toured England in 1868. The first One Day International match was played on 5 January 1971 between Australia and England at the Melbourne Cricket Ground.

In 1876–77, an England team took part in what was retrospectively recognised as the first-ever Test match at the Melbourne Cricket Ground against Australia. The rivalry between England and Australia gave birth to The Ashes in 1882, and this has remained Test cricket's most famous contest. Test cricket began to expand in 1888–89 when South Africa played England.

- World cricket in the 20th century

The inter-war years were dominated by Australia's Don Bradman, statistically the greatest Test batter of all time. Test cricket continued to expand during the 20th century with the addition of the West Indies (1928), New Zealand (1930) and India (1932) before the Second World War and then Pakistan (1952), Sri Lanka (1982), Zimbabwe (1992), Bangladesh (2000), Ireland and Afghanistan (both 2018) in the post-war period. South Africa was banned from international cricket from 1970 to 1992 as part of the apartheid boycott.

- The rise of limited overs cricket

Cricket entered a new era in 1963 when English counties introduced the limited overs variant. As it was sure to produce a result, limited overs cricket was lucrative and the number of matches increased. The first Limited Overs International was played in 1971 and the governing International Cricket Council (ICC), seeing its potential, staged the first limited overs Cricket World Cup in 1975. In the 21st century, a new limited overs form, Twenty20, made an immediate impact. On 22 June 2017, Afghanistan and Ireland became the 11th and 12th ICC full members, enabling them to play Test cricket.

- A typical cricket field.

In cricket, the rules of the game are specified in a code called The Laws of Cricket (hereinafter called "the Laws") which has a global remit. There are 42 Laws (always written with a capital "L"). The earliest known version of the code was drafted in 1744 and, since 1788, it has been owned and maintained by its custodian, the Marylebone Cricket Club (MCC) in London.

- Playing area

Cricket is a bat-and-ball game played on a cricket field between two teams of eleven players each. The field is usually circular or oval in shape and the edge of the playing area is marked by a boundary, which may be a fence, part of the stands, a rope, a painted line or a combination of these; the boundary must if possible be marked along its entire length.

In the approximate centre of the field is a rectangular pitch (see image, below) on which a wooden target called a wicket is sited at each end; the wickets are placed 22 yards (20 m) apart. The pitch is a flat surface 10 feet (3.0 m) wide, with very short grass that tends to be worn away as the game progresses (cricket can also be played on artificial surfaces, notably matting). Each wicket is made of three wooden stumps topped by two bails.

- Cricket pitch and creases

As illustrated above, the pitch is marked at each end with four white painted lines: a bowling crease, a popping crease and two return creases. The three stumps are aligned centrally on the bowling crease, which is eight feet eight inches long. The popping crease is drawn four feet in front of the bowling crease and parallel to it; although it is drawn as a twelve-foot line (six feet either side of the wicket), it is, in fact, unlimited in length. The return creases are drawn at right angles to the popping crease so that they intersect the ends of the bowling crease; each return crease is drawn as an eight-foot line, so that it extends four feet behind the bowling crease, but is also, in fact, unlimited in length.

Before a match begins, the team captains (who are also players) toss a coin to decide which team will bat first and so take the first innings. Innings is the term used for each phase of play in the match.In each innings, one team bats, attempting to score runs, while the other team bowls and fields the ball, attempting to restrict the scoring and dismiss the batters. When the first innings ends, the teams change roles; there can be two to four innings depending upon the type of match. A match with four scheduled innings is played over three to five days; a match with two scheduled innings is usually completed in a single day. During an innings, all eleven members of the fielding team take the field, but usually only two members of the batting team are on the field at any given time.

The exception to this is if a batter has any type of illness or injury restricting his or her ability to run, in this case the batter is allowed a runner who can run between the wickets when the batter hits a scoring run or runs,though this does not apply in international cricket. The order of batters is usually announced just before the match, but it can be varied.

The main objective of each team is to score more runs than their opponents but, in some forms of cricket, it is also necessary to dismiss all of the opposition batters in their final innings in order to win the match, which would otherwise be drawn. If the team batting last is all out having scored fewer runs than their opponents, they are said to have "lost by n runs" (where n is the difference between the aggregate number of runs scored by the teams). If the team that bats last scores enough runs to win, it is said to have "won by n wickets", where n is the number of wickets left to fall. For example, a team that passes its opponents‘ total having lost six wickets (i.e., six of their batters have been dismissed) have won the match "by four wickets".

In a two-innings-a-side match, one team's combined first and second innings total may be less than the other side's first innings total. The team with the greater score is then said to have "won by an innings and n runs", and does not need to bat again: n is the difference between the two teams' aggregate scores. If the team batting last is all out, and both sides have scored the same number of runs, then the match is a tie; this result is quite rare in matches of two innings a side with only 62 happening in first-class matches from the earliest known instance in 1741 until January 2017. In the traditional form of the game, if the time allotted for the match expires before either side can win, then the game is declared a draw.

If the match has only a single innings per side, then a maximum number of overs applies to each innings. Such a match is called a "limited overs" or "one-day" match, and the side scoring more runs wins regardless of the number of wickets lost, so that a draw cannot occur. In some cases, ties are broken by having each team bat for a one-over innings known as a Super Over; subsequent Super Overs may be played if the first Super Over ends in a tie. If this kind of match is temporarily interrupted by bad weather, then a complex mathematical formula, known as the Duckworth–Lewis–Stern method after its developers, is often used to recalculate a new target score. A one-day match can also be declared a "no-result" if fewer than a previously agreed number of overs have been bowled by either team, in circumstances that make normal resumption of play impossible; for example, wet weather.

In all forms of cricket, the umpires can abandon the match if bad light or rain makes it impossible to continue. There have been instances of entire matches, even Test matches scheduled to be played over five days, being lost to bad weather without a ball being bowled: for example, the third Test of the 1970/71 series in Australia.

- Innings

The innings (ending with 's' in both singular and plural form) is the term used for each phase of play during a match. Depending on the type of match being played, each team has either one or two innings. Sometimes all eleven members of the batting side take a turn to bat but, for various reasons, an innings can end before they have all done so. The innings terminates if the batting team is "all out", a term defined by the Laws: "at the fall of a wicket or the retirement of a batter, further balls remain to be bowled but no further batter is available to come in". In this situation, one of the batters has not been dismissed and is termed not out; this is because he has no partners left and there must always be two active batters while the innings is in progress.

- An innings may end early while there are still two not out batters

the batting team's captain may declare the innings closed even though some of his players have not had a turn to bat: this is a tactical decision by the captain, usually because he believes his team have scored sufficient runs and need time to dismiss the opposition in their innings

the set number of overs (i.e., in a limited overs match) have been bowled

the match has ended prematurely due to bad weather or running out of time

in the final innings of the match, the batting side has reached its target and won the game.

- Overs

The Laws state that, throughout an innings, "the ball shall be bowled from each end alternately in overs of 6 balls". The name "over" came about because the umpire calls "Over!" when six balls have been bowled. At this point, another bowler is deployed at the other end, and the fielding side changes ends while the batters do not. A bowler cannot bowl two successive overs, although a bowler can (and usually does) bowl alternate overs, from the same end, for several overs which are termed a "spell". The batters do not change ends at the end of the over, and so the one who was non-striker is now the striker and vice versa. The umpires also change positions so that the one who was at "square leg" now stands behind the wicket at the non-striker's end and vice versa.

- Clothing and equipment

English cricketer W. G. Grace "taking guard" in 1883. His pads and bat are very similar to those used today. The gloves have evolved somewhat. Many modern players use more defensive equipment than were available to Grace, most notably helmets and arm guards.

The wicket-keeper (a specialised fielder behind the batter) and the batters wear protective gear because of the hardness of the ball, which can be delivered at speeds of more than 145 kilometres per hour (90 mph) and presents a major health and safety concern.

Protective clothing includes pads (designed to protect the knees and shins), batting gloves or wicket-keeper's gloves for the hands, a safety helmet for the head and a box for male players inside the trousers (to protect the crotch area). Some batters wear additional padding inside their shirts and trousers such as thigh pads, arm pads, rib protectors and shoulder pads. The only fielders allowed to wear protective gear are those in positions very close to the batter (i.e., if they are alongside or in front of him), but they cannot wear gloves or external leg guards.

Subject to certain variations, on-field clothing generally includes a collared shirt with short or long sleeves; long trousers; woolen pullover (if needed); cricket cap (for fielding) or a safety helmet; and spiked shoes or boots to increase traction. The kit is traditionally all white and this remains the case in Test and first-class cricket but, in limited overs cricket, team colours are worn instead.

- Bat and ball

Two types of cricket ball, both of the same size:

i) A used white ball. White balls are mainly used in limited overs cricket, especially in matches played at night, under floodlights (left).

ii) A used red ball. Red balls are used in Test cricket, first-class cricket and some other forms of cricket (right).

The essence of the sport is that a bowler delivers (i.e., bowls) the ball from his or her end of the pitch towards the batter who, armed with a bat, is "on strike" at the other end (see next sub-section: Basic gameplay).

The bat is made of wood, usually Salix alba (white willow), and has the shape of a blade topped by a cylindrical handle. The blade must not be more than 4.25 inches (10.8 cm) wide and the total length of the bat not more than 38 inches (97 cm). There is no standard for the weight, which is usually between 2 lb 7 oz and 3 lb (1.1 and 1.4 kg).

The ball is a hard leather-seamed spheroid, with a circumference of 9 inches (23 cm). The ball has a "seam": six rows of stitches attaching the leather shell of the ball to the string and cork interior. The seam on a new ball is prominent and helps the bowler propel it in a less predictable manner. During matches, the quality of the ball deteriorates to a point where it is no longer usable; during the course of this deterioration, its behaviour in flight will change and can influence the outcome of the match. Players will, therefore, attempt to modify the ball's behaviour by modifying its physical properties. Polishing the ball and wetting it with sweat or saliva is legal, even when the polishing is deliberately done on one side only to increase the ball's swing through the air, but the acts of rubbing other substances into the ball, scratching the surface or picking at the seam are illegal ball tampering.

- Player roles

Basic gameplay: bowler to batter

During normal play, thirteen players and two umpires are on the field. Two of the players are batters and the rest are all eleven members of the fielding team. The other nine players in the batting team are off the field in the pavilion. The image with overlay below shows what is happening when a ball is being bowled and which of the personnel are on or close to the pitch.

- Return crease

In the photo, the two batters (3 & 8; wearing yellow) have taken position at each end of the pitch (6). Three members of the fielding team (4, 10 & 11; wearing dark blue) are in shot. One of the two umpires (1; wearing white hat) is stationed behind the wicket (2) at the bowler's (4) end of the pitch. The bowler (4) is bowling the ball (5) from his end of the pitch to the batter at the other end who is called the "striker". The other batter (3) at the bowling end is called the "non-striker". The wicket-keeper (10), who is a specialist, is positioned behind the striker's wicket (9) and behind him stands one of the fielders in a position called "first slip" (11). While the bowler and the first slip are wearing conventional kit only, the two batters and the wicket-keeper are wearing protective gear including safety helmets, padded gloves and leg guards (pads).

While the umpire (1) in shot stands at the bowler's end of the pitch, his colleague stands in the outfield, usually in or near the fielding position called "square leg", so that he is in line with the popping crease (7) at the striker's end of the pitch. The bowling crease (not numbered) is the one on which the wicket is located between the return creases (12). The bowler (4) intends to hit the wicket (9) with the ball (5) or, at least, to prevent the striker (8) from scoring runs. The striker (8) intends, by using his bat, to defend his wicket and, if possible, to hit the ball away from the pitch in order to score runs.

Some players are skilled in both batting and bowling, or as either or these as well as wicket-keeping, so are termed all-rounders. Bowlers are classified according to their style, generally as fast bowlers, seam bowlers or spinners. Batters are classified according to whether they are right-handed or left-handed.

- Fielding

Of the eleven fielders, three are in shot in the image above. The other eight are elsewhere on the field, their positions determined on a tactical basis by the captain or the bowler. Fielders often change position between deliveries, again as directed by the captain or bowler.

If a fielder is injured or becomes ill during a match, a substitute is allowed to field instead of him, but the substitute cannot bowl or act as a captain, except in the case of concussion substitutes in international cricket. The substitute leaves the field when the injured player is fit to return. The Laws of Cricket were updated in 2017 to allow substitutes to act as wicket-keepers.

- Bowling and dismissal

Glenn McGrath of Australia holds the world record for most wickets in the Cricket World Cup.

Most bowlers are considered specialists in that they are selected for the team because of their skill as a bowler, although some are all-rounders and even specialist batters bowl occasionally. The specialists bowl several times during an innings but may not bowl two overs consecutively. If the captain wants a bowler to "change ends", another bowler must temporarily fill in so that the change is not immediate.

A bowler reaches his delivery stride by means of a "run-up" and an over is deemed to have begun when the bowler starts his run-up for the first delivery of that over, the ball then being "in play".

Fast bowlers, needing momentum, take a lengthy run up while bowlers with a slow delivery take no more than a couple of steps before bowling. The fastest bowlers can deliver the ball at a speed of over 145 kilometres per hour (90 mph) and they sometimes rely on sheer speed to try to defeat the batter, who is forced to react very quickly.

Other fast bowlers rely on a mixture of speed and guile by making the ball seam or swing (i.e. curve) in flight. This type of delivery can deceive a batter into miscuing his shot, for example, so that the ball just touches the edge of the bat and can then be "caught behind" by the wicket-keeper or a slip fielder. At the other end of the bowling scale is the spin bowler who bowls at a relatively slow pace and relies entirely on guile to deceive the batter. A spinner will often "buy his wicket" by "tossing one up" (in a slower, steeper parabolic path) to lure the batter into making a poor shot. The batter has to be very wary of such deliveries as they are often "flighted" or spun so that the ball will not behave quite as he expects and he could be "trapped" into getting himself out. In between the pacemen and the spinners are the medium paced seamers who rely on persistent accuracy to try to contain the rate of scoring and wear down the batter's concentration.

There are nine ways in which a batter can be dismissed: five relatively common and four extremely rare. The common forms of dismissal are bowled, caught, leg before wicket (lbw), run out and stumped. Rare methods are hit wicket,hit the ball twice, obstructing the field and timed out. The Laws state that the fielding team, usually the bowler in practice, must appeal for a dismissal before the umpire can give his decision. If the batter is out, the umpire raises a forefinger and says "Out!"; otherwise, he will shake his head and say "Not out".There is, effectively, a tenth method of dismissal, retired out, which is not an on-field dismissal as such but rather a retrospective one for which no fielder is credited.

- Batting, runs and extras

The directions in which a right-handed batter, facing down the page, intends to send the ball when playing various cricketing shots. The diagram for a left-handed batter is a mirror image of this one.

Batters take turns to bat via a batting order which is decided beforehand by the team captain and presented to the umpires, though the order remains flexible when the captain officially nominates the team. Substitute batters are generally not allowed, except in the case of concussion substitutes in international cricket.

In order to begin batting the batter first adopts a batting stance. Standardly, this involves adopting a slight crouch with the feet pointing across the front of the wicket, looking in the direction of the bowler, and holding the bat so it passes over the feet and so its tip can rest on the ground near to the toes of the back foot.

A skilled batter can use a wide array of "shots" or "strokes" in both defensive and attacking mode. The idea is to hit the ball to the best effect with the flat surface of the bat's blade. If the ball touches the side of the bat it is called an "edge". The batter does not have to play a shot and can allow the ball to go through to the wicketkeeper. Equally, he does not have to attempt a run when he hits the ball with his bat. Batters do not always seek to hit the ball as hard as possible, and a good player can score runs just by making a deft stroke with a turn of the wrists or by simply "blocking" the ball but directing it away from fielders so that he has time to take a run. A wide variety of shots are played, the batter's repertoire including strokes named according to the style of swing and the direction aimed: e.g., "cut", "drive", "hook", "pull".

The batter on strike (i.e. the "striker") must prevent the ball hitting the wicket, and try to score runs by hitting the ball with his bat so that he and his partner have time to run from one end of the pitch to the other before the fielding side can return the ball. To register a run, both runners must touch the ground behind the popping crease with either their bats or their bodies (the batters carry their bats as they run). Each completed run increments the score of both the team and the striker.

- Sachin Tendulkar is the only player to have scored one hundred international centuries

The decision to attempt a run is ideally made by the batter who has the better view of the ball's progress, and this is communicated by calling: usually "yes", "no" or "wait". More than one run can be scored from a single hit: hits worth one to three runs are common, but the size of the field is such that it is usually difficult to run four or more. To compensate for this, hits that reach the boundary of the field are automatically awarded four runs if the ball touches the ground en route to the boundary or six runs if the ball clears the boundary without touching the ground within the boundary. In these cases the batters do not need to run. Hits for five are unusual and generally rely on the help of "overthrows" by a fielder returning the ball. If an odd number of runs is scored by the striker, the two batters have changed ends, and the one who was non-striker is now the striker. Only the striker can score individual runs, but all runs are added to the team's total.

Additional runs can be gained by the batting team as extras (called "sundries" in Australia) due to errors made by the fielding side. This is achieved in four ways: no-ball, a penalty of one extra conceded by the bowler if he breaks the rules; wide, a penalty of one extra conceded by the bowler if he bowls so that the ball is out of the batter's reach bye, an extra awarded if the batter misses the ball and it goes past the wicket-keeper and gives the batters time to run in the conventional way leg bye, as for a bye except that the ball has hit the batter's body, though not his bat. If the bowler has conceded a no-ball or a wide, his team incurs an additional penalty because that ball (i.e., delivery) has to be bowled again and hence the batting side has the opportunity to score more runs from this extra ball.

- Specialist roles

Captain (cricket) and Wicket-keeper

The captain is often the most experienced player in the team, certainly the most tactically astute, and can possess any of the main skillsets as a batter, a bowler or a wicket-keeper. Within the Laws, the captain has certain responsibilities in terms of nominating his players to the umpires before the match and ensuring that his players conduct themselves "within the spirit and traditions of the game as well as within the Laws".

The wicket-keeper (sometimes called simply the "keeper") is a specialist fielder subject to various rules within the Laws about his equipment and demeanour. He is the only member of the fielding side who can effect a stumping and is the only one permitted to wear gloves and external leg guards. Depending on their primary skills, the other ten players in the team tend to be classified as specialist batters or specialist bowlers. Generally, a team will include five or six specialist batters and four or five specialist bowlers, plus the wicket-keeper.

- Umpires and scorers

Umpire (cricket), Scoring (cricket), and Cricket statistics

An umpire signals a decision to the scorers

The game on the field is regulated by the two umpires, one of whom stands behind the wicket at the bowler's end, the other in a position called "square leg" which is about 15–20 metres away from the batter on strike and in line with the popping crease on which he is taking guard. The umpires have several responsibilities including adjudication on whether a ball has been correctly bowled (i.e., not a no-ball or a wide); when a run is scored; whether a batter is out (the fielding side must first appeal to the umpire, usually with the phrase "How's that?" or "Owzat?"); when intervals start and end; and the suitability of the pitch, field and weather for playing the game. The umpires are authorised to interrupt or even abandon a match due to circumstances likely to endanger the players, such as a damp pitch or deterioration of the light.

Off the field in televised matches, there is usually a third umpire who can make decisions on certain incidents with the aid of video evidence. The third umpire is mandatory under the playing conditions for Test and Limited Overs International matches played between two ICC full member countries. These matches also have a match referee whose job is to ensure that play is within the Laws and the spirit of the game.

The match details, including runs and dismissals, are recorded by two official scorers, one representing each team. The scorers are directed by the hand signals of an umpire . For example, the umpire raises a forefinger to signal that the batter is out (has been dismissed); he raises both arms above his head if the batter has hit the ball for six runs. The scorers are required by the Laws to record all runs scored, wickets taken and overs bowled; in practice, they also note significant amounts of additional data relating to the game.

A match's statistics are summarised on a scorecard. Prior to the popularisation of scorecards, most scoring was done by men sitting on vantage points cuttings notches on tally sticks and runs were originally called notches.According to Rowland Bowen, the earliest known scorecard templates were introduced in 1776 by T. Pratt of Sevenoaks and soon came into general use.It is believed that scorecards were printed and sold at Lord's for the first time in 1846.

- *thank you for buy & read this book*

have a great day of your
from : Mr Vivek Kumar Pandey

Printed by Libri Plureos GmbH in Hamburg,
Germany